# INTRODUCTION

Read all instructions before you begin.

## Materials

All of the paper materials you will need for the eight planes in this book — *Daedalus, Icarus, Songbird, Baker F-399, Baker X-411, Pegasus, Phantom,* and *Stratospheron* — are included on the following pages. To construct the planes you will also require the following:

Scissors or a matte knife (such as that made by the X-ACTO company)
White glue
½" brush or a piece of index card cut to ½" to spread glue
Paper clips
Ruler
Scoring tool or sharp pencil
Transparent tape (*not* the "invisible" kind)
One penny for each plane

## Assembling the Airplanes

The paper materials appear on either three or four pages for each plane. All the pieces are clearly identified. Since the planes are brightly colored on all sides (e.g., both the top and bottom of the wings), most of the pages are printed on both sides. (There is an exception to this: on page 31 appear the fuselage reinforcement and rudder pieces for *Phantom* and *Stratospheron.* The designs of these pieces — they fit in their entirety within other pieces — do not require printing on two sides, therefore page 32 is blank. Also, the wing braces for all eight planes are printed only on one side.) You only need to follow the guidelines on the top or front sides of each page to cut out the planes. *Do not cut out the pieces from the back.* The backs of the pieces have been printed larger than the fronts to insure that, when you cut out the fronts, the color on the backs will extend to the very edge of every visible part. All of the plates clearly indicate which side of the sheet of paper you should be cutting from.

1. Cut out the main piece of the airplane and the fuselage reinforcement and rudder piece. Score the fold lines on both pieces with the scoring tool or sharp pencil and ruler. On the main piece, fold the fuselage together on the broken line and the wings down on the dotted lines (see Figure 1). Fold the fuselage reinforcement and rudder piece up on the dashed lines.

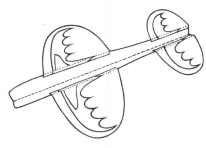

**Figure 1.** The folded airplane.

2. Spread glue thinly on the inside of the fuselage reinforcement and rudder piece (being careful not to put glue on the rudder) and on the penny. Place the penny where indicated and close the fuselage reinforcement piece, securing it with paper clips (see Figure 2). Let the glue dry — about 4–5 minutes.

**Figure 2.** The folded and glued fuselage reinforcement and rudder piece, held together with paper clips.

3. Spread glue thinly on the outside of the dry fuselage reinforcement and rudder piece, avoiding putting glue on the rudder itself, and spread glue on the inside of the fuselage on the main piece of the airplane. Let dry for a minute until slightly tacky, and then place the fuselage reinforcement and rudder piece inside the fuselage of the main piece with the rudder at the back. Close the fuselage and secure it with paper clips (see Figure 3). Let the glue dry thoroughly.

**Figure 3.** The fuselage reinforcement and rudder piece placed inside the fuselage and secured with paper clips.

4. Cut out the wing brace and spread glue on the bottom or back side (i.e., the side with no color). Note that there are lines — position lines — on the top of the wings that correspond to the shape of the wing brace. Holding the wings at 90° angles to the fuselage, place the wing brace over the position lines, covering the lines completely and pressing down to insure that the glue binds the pieces together securely. Hold the pieces in place by hand until dry (3–4 minutes), and then bend the wings up slightly to the dihedral angle shown for the particular airplane (see Figure 4).

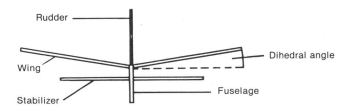

**Figure 4.** Front view of airplane showing dihedral angle of wings.

5. The stabilizers should be at a 90° angle to the fuselage except for *Phantom* and *Stratospheron,* in which cases

they are at the top of the rudder and must be bent down slightly. Strengthen the stabilizers with a piece of tape on the fold (see Figure 5). Apply the tape under the stabilizers *after* they have been folded to the correct position. Tape should also be used in the same manner to reinforce the wings, and the stabilizers for *Phantom* and *Stratospheron* should be strengthened with a piece of tape across the top joining surface. The nose of the airplane may be wrapped in tape for extra strength.

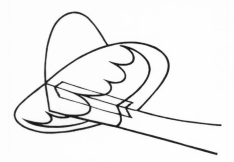

**Figure 5.** Tape applied underneath the stabilizer.

## Adjusting and Flying the Airplanes

**1.** Before you start flying your airplane, there are two important checks to be made. First, make sure that both sides of the airplane are exactly the same — both wings at the same angle, and both stabilizers the same. Then check the center of gravity by balancing the airplane on the index fingers of both hands. Place your fingers, one on each side of the fuselage, slightly behind the center of the wings next to the fuselage. When in balance the airplane should lie parallel to the ground. If it falls back toward the tail and does not glide well, it may need a paper clip on the nose. Test-glide it several times, adjusting the position of the paper clip (closer to or farther from the nose) until the airplane flies correctly.

**2.** Test-glide the airplane by gently launching it at chest height, holding the fuselage under the wings (see Figure 6). If the airplane falls down nose first, gently curl the aile-

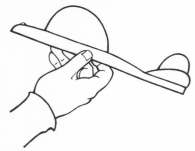

**Figure 6.** Holding the airplane before a launch.

ron areas of the wings down slightly, and curl the elevator areas on the stabilizers up slightly to give the airplane more lift (see Figure 7). Test-glide the plane several times, with slight variations each time in the amount of curl in the wings and stabilizers, until the adjustments are correct. If the airplane veers sharply to the left or right, compare the front view of the plane with the illustration in the book to see that both sides of the airplane are properly aligned. If the airplane still turns to one side after being realigned, try turning the back edge of the rudder in the opposite direction of the flight; for example, if the airplane turns right, bend the rudder slightly to the left. Practice for a while with gentle throws until you can get an

even, controlled glide (see Figure 8). If you are launching too fast, the airplane will go up sharply and then fall down; if the launch is too slow, the airplane will just fall down.

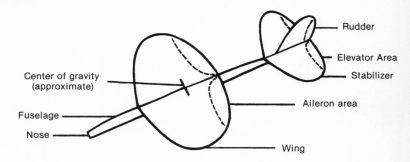

**Figure 7.** The parts of an airplane.

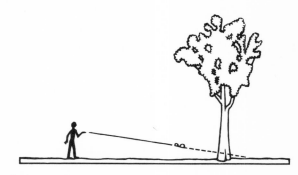

**Figure 8.** A test glide.

**3.** When the airplane is correctly adjusted for short flights, you are ready for high flights. It is best to fly the airplane in a large open place such as a park or an athletic field. Hold the airplane under the wings as shown in Figure 6, and then throw it upward at a steep angle (see Figure 9). The airplane should go as high as a telephone pole or tall tree, and level off at that height before gradually gliding to the ground. It can travel a considerable distance when it is in the air.

If you throw it up and it goes high but does not level off and nose-dives instead, try curling the ailerons down and the elevators up. To make the plane circle when it is high, turn the back edge of the rudder toward the direction you want it to go — for example, to circle right, turn the rudder right. Adjust the amount of curl in the ailerons, elevators, and rudder over several flights until it flies the way you want it to.

An excellent book on adjusting and flying paper airplanes is *How to Make and Fly Paper Airplanes* by Captain Ralph S. Barnaby, U.S. Navy (Ret.), (New York: Four Winds Press, 1968).

**Figure 9.** Throwing the plane upward at a steep angle.

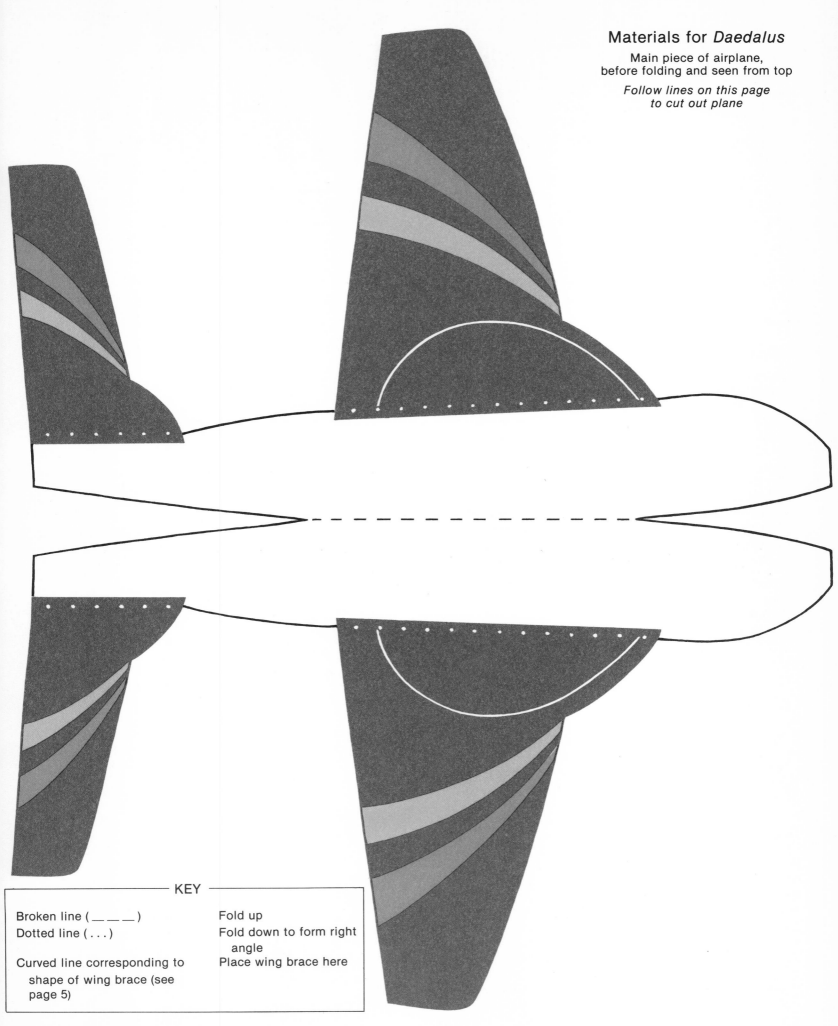

## Materials for *Daedalus*

Main piece of airplane,
before folding and seen from top

*Follow lines on this page
to cut out plane*

--- KEY ---

Broken line ( _ _ _ )                          Fold up
Dotted line ( . . . )                          Fold down to form right
                                                   angle
Curved line corresponding to         Place wing brace here
   shape of wing brace (see
   page 5)

**Materials for _Daedalus_**

Underside of main piece of plane
before folding. _Cut out this piece by_
_following lines on preceding page_

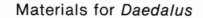

# Materials for *Daedalus*

*Follow lines on this page to cut out the wing brace and the fuselage reinforcement and rudder piece.*

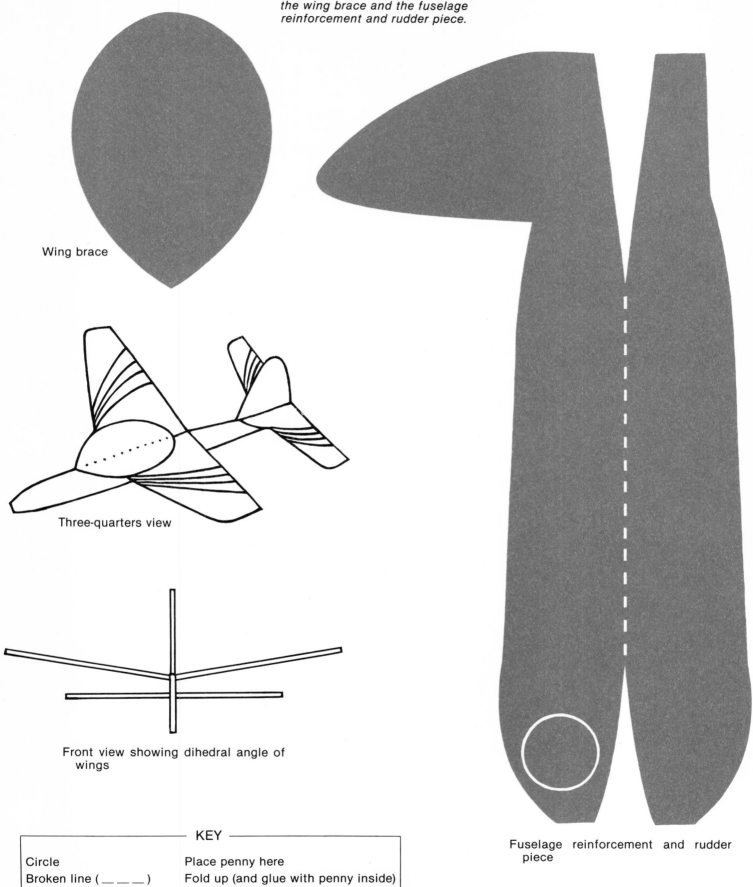

Wing brace

Three-quarters view

Front view showing dihedral angle of
wings

Fuselage reinforcement and rudder
piece

──────── KEY ────────

Circle — Place penny here

Broken line ( _ _ _ ) — Fold up (and glue with penny inside)

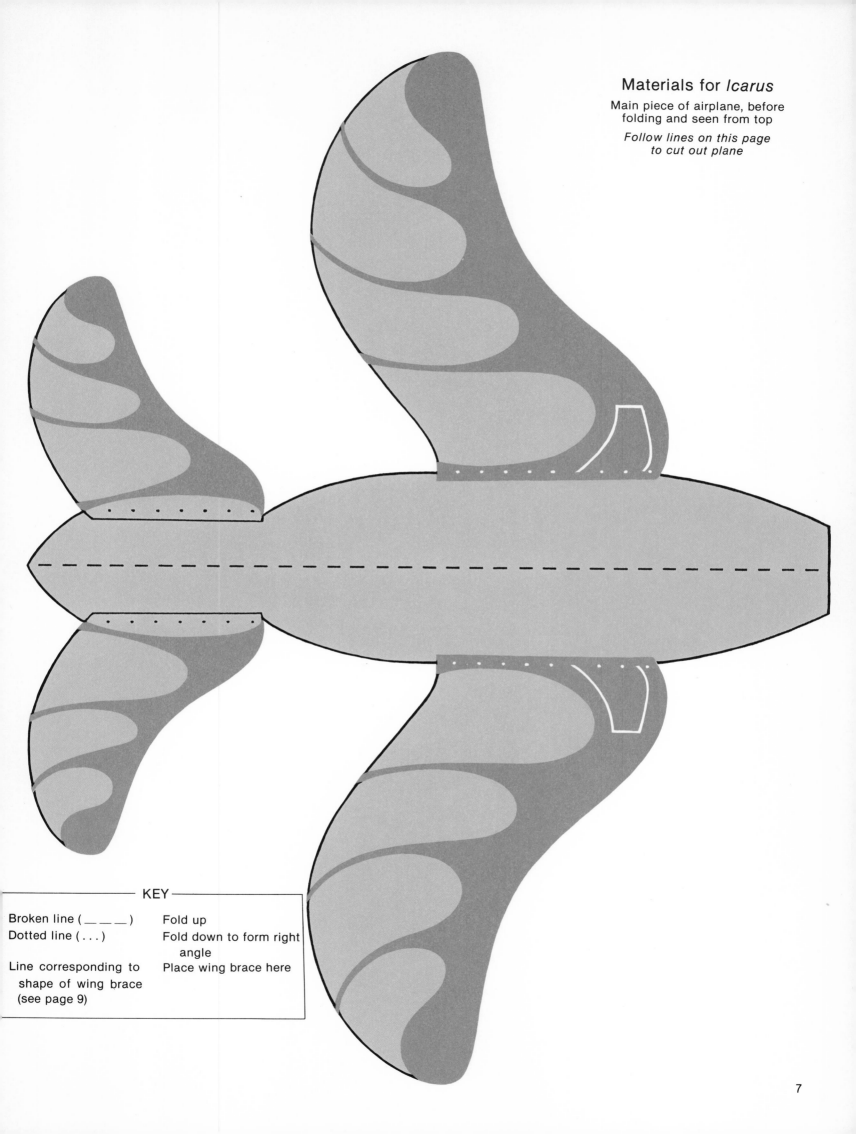

## Materials for *Icarus*

Main piece of airplane, before folding and seen from top

*Follow lines on this page to cut out plane*

—————— KEY ——————

Broken line (_ _ _)          Fold up
Dotted line ( . . . )         Fold down to form right angle
                              Place wing brace here
Line corresponding to
   shape of wing brace
   (see page 9)

### Materials for *Icarus*

Underside of main piece of airplane before folding.
*Cut out this piece by following lines on preceding pag*

# Materials for *Icarus*

*Cut out wing brace and fuselage reinforcement
and rudder piece by following lines on this page*

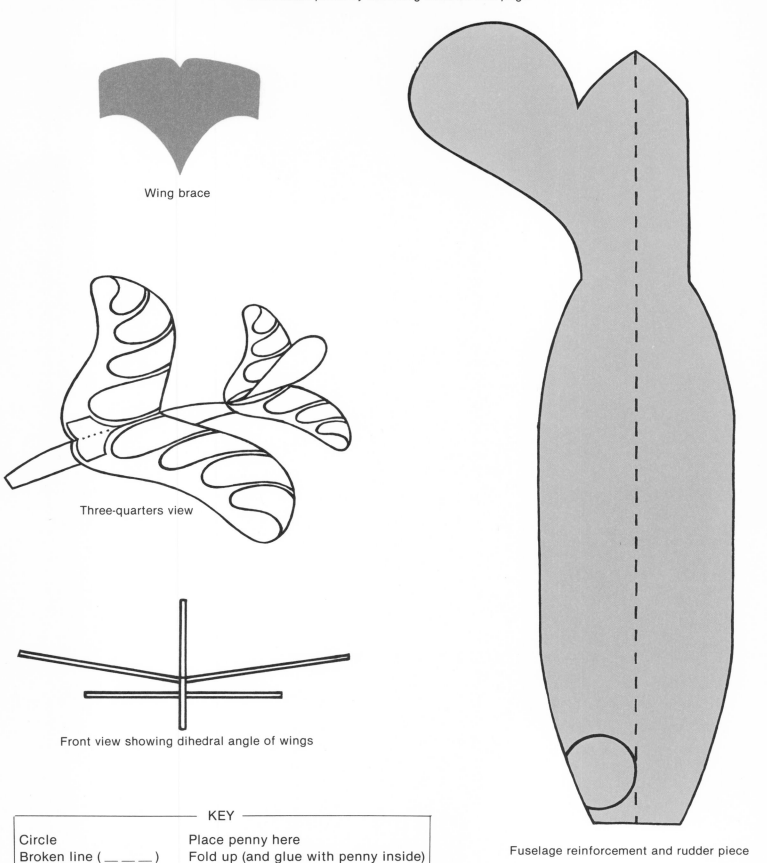

Wing brace

Three-quarters view

Front view showing dihedral angle of wings

| — KEY — | |
|---|---|
| Circle | Place penny here |
| Broken line ( _ _ _ ) | Fold up (and glue with penny inside) |

Fuselage reinforcement and rudder piece

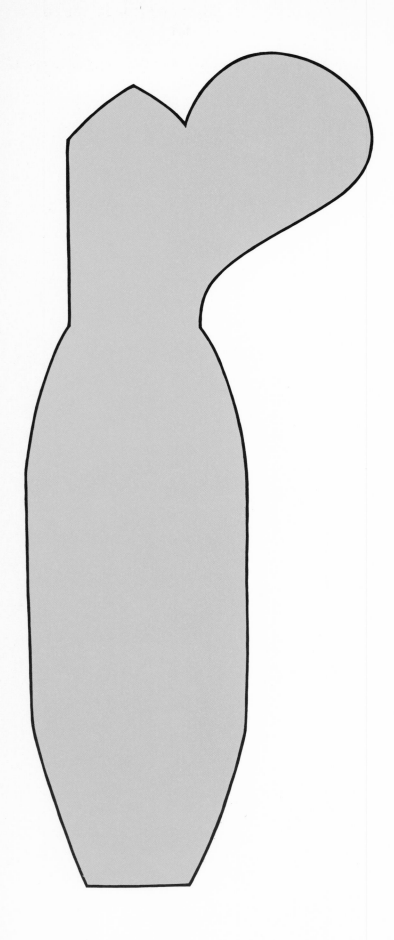

## Materials for *Icarus*
Fuselage reinforcement and rudder piece.
*Cut out this piece by following lines on preceding page*

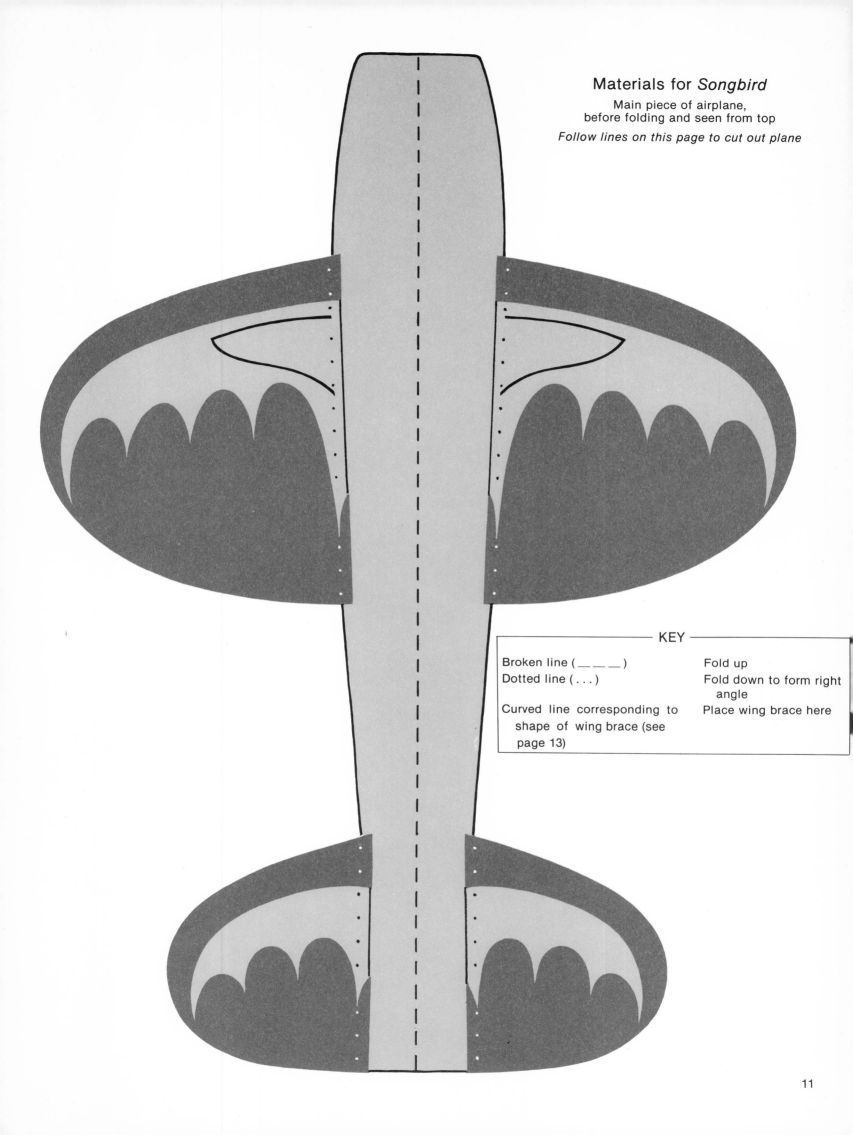

## Materials for *Songbird*

Main piece of airplane,
before folding and seen from top

*Follow lines on this page to cut out plane*

───── KEY ─────

Broken line ( ___ ___ ___ )            Fold up

Dotted line ( . . . )                          Fold down to form right
                                                          angle

Curved line corresponding to       Place wing brace here
   shape of wing brace (see
   page 13)

## Materials for *Songbird*

Underside of main piece of airplane before folding.
*Cut out this piece by following lines on preceding page*

## Materials for *Songbird*

*Follow lines on this page to cut out the wing brace and the fuselage reinforcement and rudder piece*

Wing brace

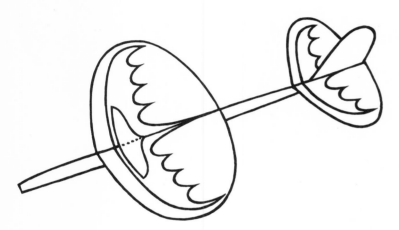

Three-quarters view

Front view showing dihedral angle of wings

Fuselage reinforcement
and rudder piece

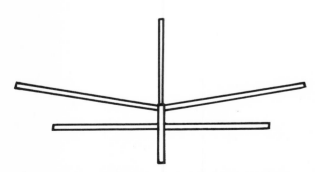

| KEY | |
|---|---|
| Circle | Place penny here |
| Broken line ( _ _ _ ) | Fold up (and glue with penny inside) |

## Materials for *Songbird*
Fuselage reinforcement and rudder piece.
*Cut out this piece by following lines on preceding page*

## Materials for *Baker F-399*

Main piece of airplane, before folding and seen from top

*Follow lines on this page to cut out plane*

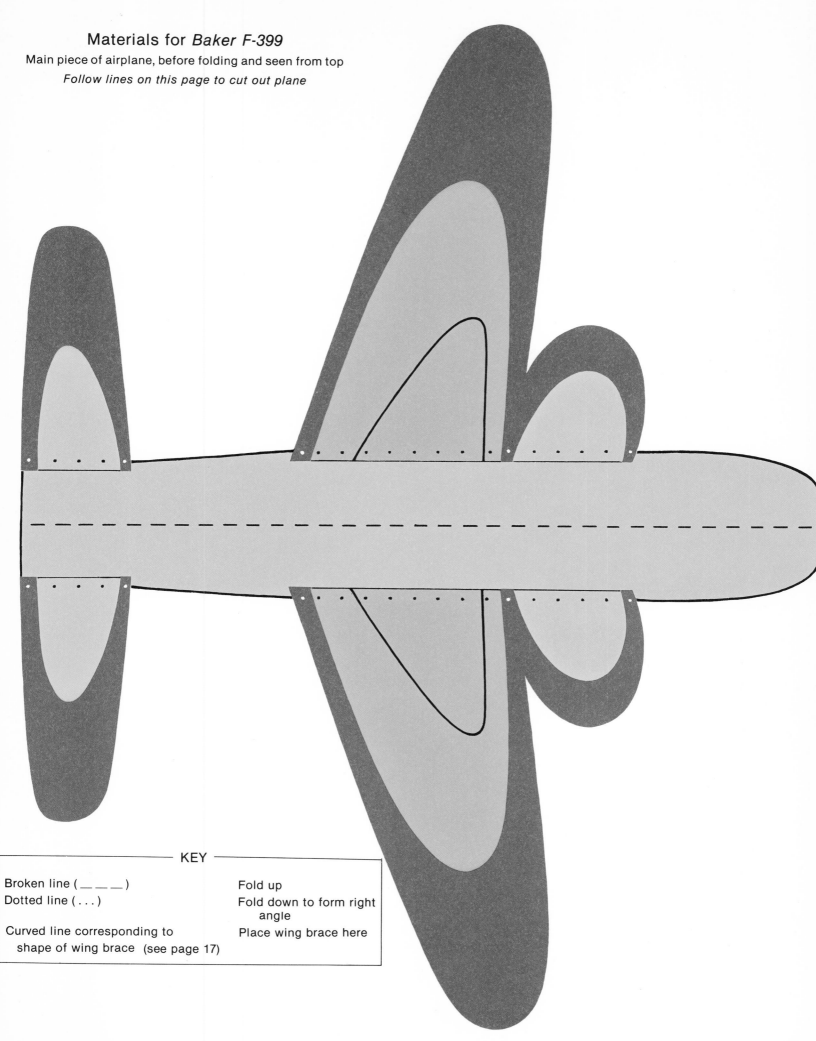

───── KEY ─────

Broken line ( __ __ __ )        Fold up

Dotted line ( . . . )        Fold down to form right
                                 angle

Curved line corresponding to        Place wing brace here
  shape of wing brace  (see page 17)

Underside of main piece of
plane before folding. *Cut out
this piece by following lines
on preceding page*

## Materials for *Baker F-399*

*Follow lines on this page to cut out the wing brace and the fuselage reinforcement and rudder piece*

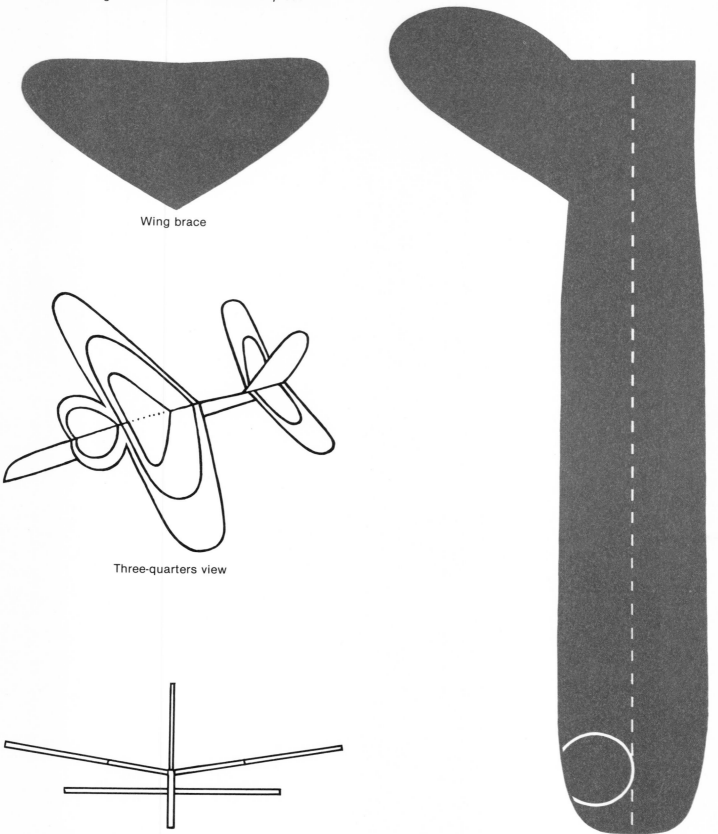

Wing brace

Three-quarters view

Front view showing dihedral angle of wings

Fuselage reinforcement and rudder piece

| KEY | |
|---|---|
| Circle | Place penny here |
| Broken line ( _ _ _ ) | Fold up (and glue with penny inside) |

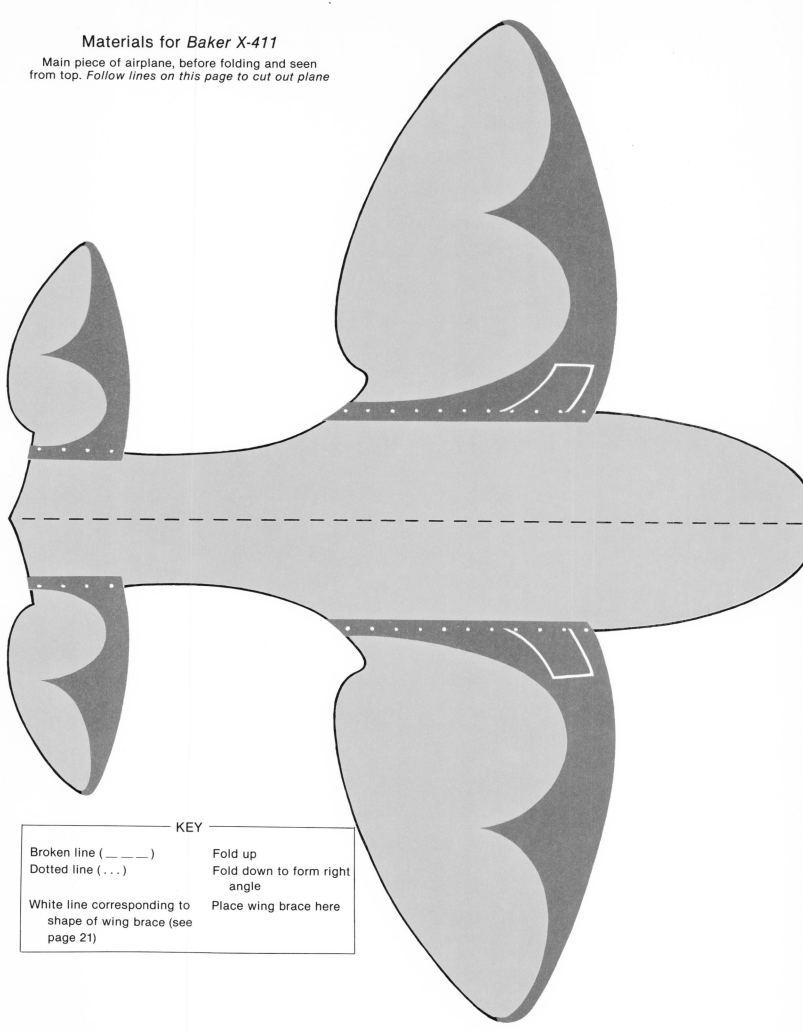

## Materials for *Baker X-411*

Main piece of airplane, before folding and seen from top. *Follow lines on this page to cut out plane*

─── KEY ───

Broken line ( _ _ _ )                    Fold up

Dotted line ( . . . )                      Fold down to form right
                                                      angle

White line corresponding to        Place wing brace here
    shape of wing brace (see
    page 21)

**Materials for** *Baker X-411*

Underside of main piece of plane
before folding. *Cut out this piece
by following lines on preceding page*

# Materials for *Baker X-411*

*Follow lines on this page to cut out the wing brace
and the fuselage reinforcement and rudder piece*

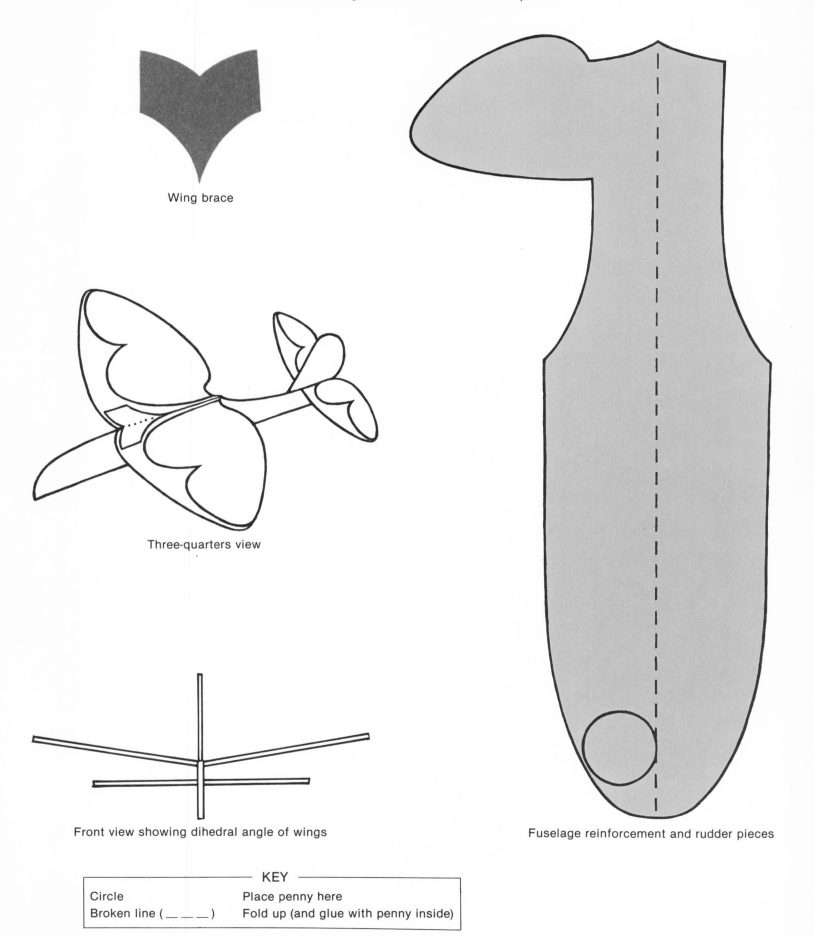

Wing brace

Three-quarters view

Front view showing dihedral angle of wings

Fuselage reinforcement and rudder pieces

| KEY | |
|---|---|
| Circle | Place penny here |
| Broken line ( _ _ _ ) | Fold up (and glue with penny inside) |

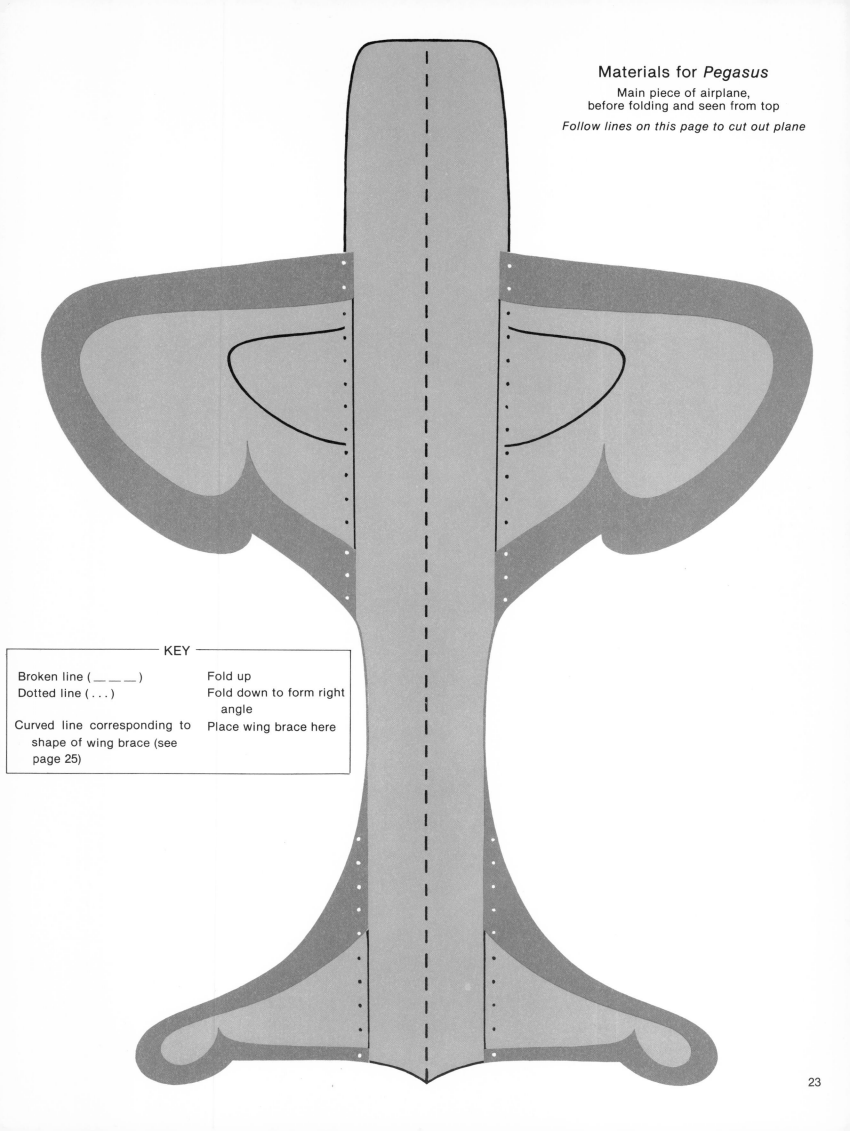

KEY

Broken line ( _ _ _ )  Fold up
Dotted line ( . . . )  Fold down to form right
angle

Curved line corresponding to  Place wing brace here
shape of wing brace (see
page 25)

**Materials for _Pegasus_**
Underside of main piece of plane.
_Cut out this piece by following
lines on preceding page_

## Materials for *Pegasus*

*Follow lines on this page to cut out the wing brace and the fuselage reinforcement and rudder piece*

Wing brace

Fuselage reinforcement
and rudder pieces

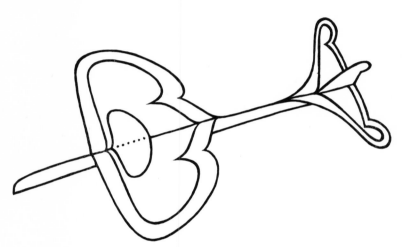

Three-quarters view

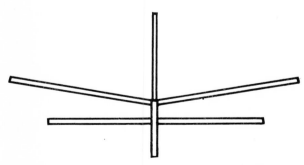

Front view showing dihedral angle of wings

| KEY | |
|---|---|
| White circle | Place penny here |
| Broken line ( _ _ _ ) | Fold up (and glue with penny inside) |

## Materials for *Pegasus*
Fuselage reinforcement and rudder piece.
*Cut out this piece by following lines on preceding page*

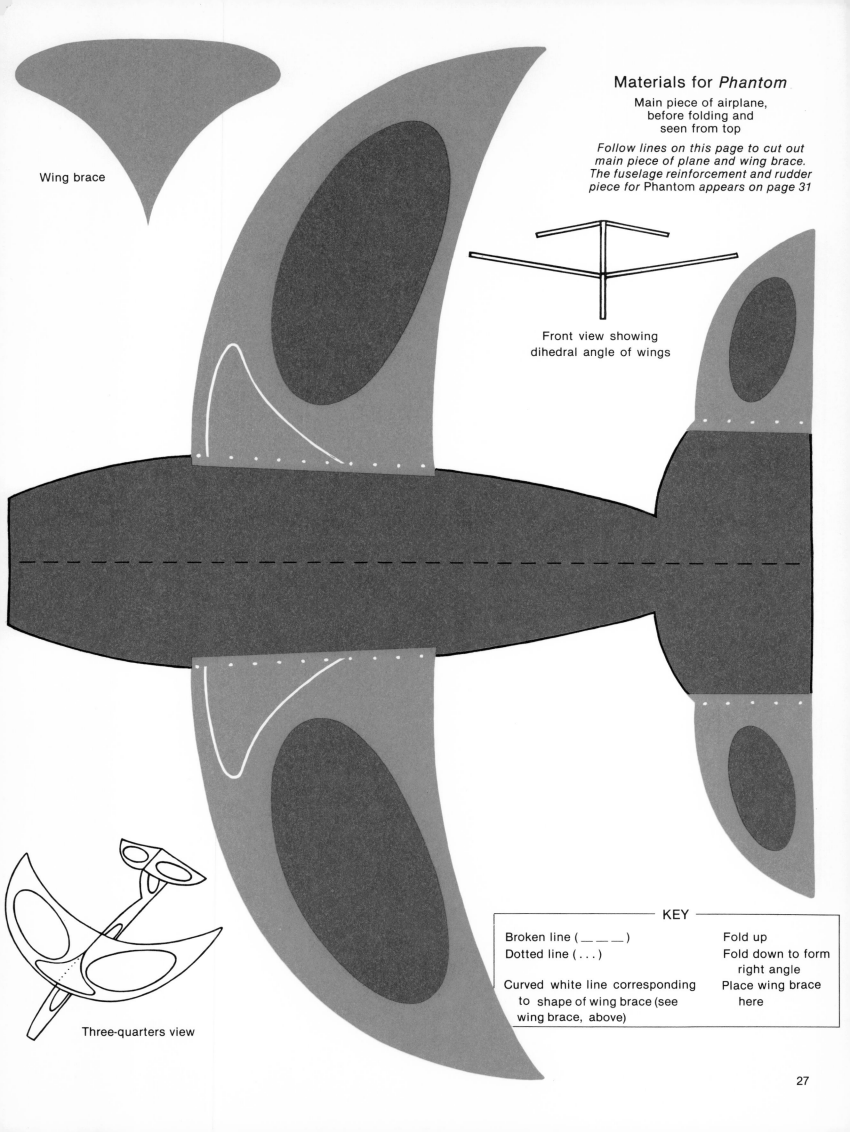

Wing brace

## Materials for *Phantom*

Main piece of airplane,
before folding and
seen from top

*Follow lines on this page to cut out
main piece of plane and wing brace.
The fuselage reinforcement and rudder
piece for* Phantom *appears on page 31*

Front view showing
dihedral angle of wings

Three-quarters view

### KEY

Broken line ( _ _ _ )          Fold up

Dotted line ( . . . )          Fold down to form
                               right angle

Curved white line corresponding    Place wing brace
  to shape of wing brace (see       here
  wing brace, above)

**Materials for *Phantom***

Underside of main piece of plane before folding. *Cut out this piece by following lines on preceding page*

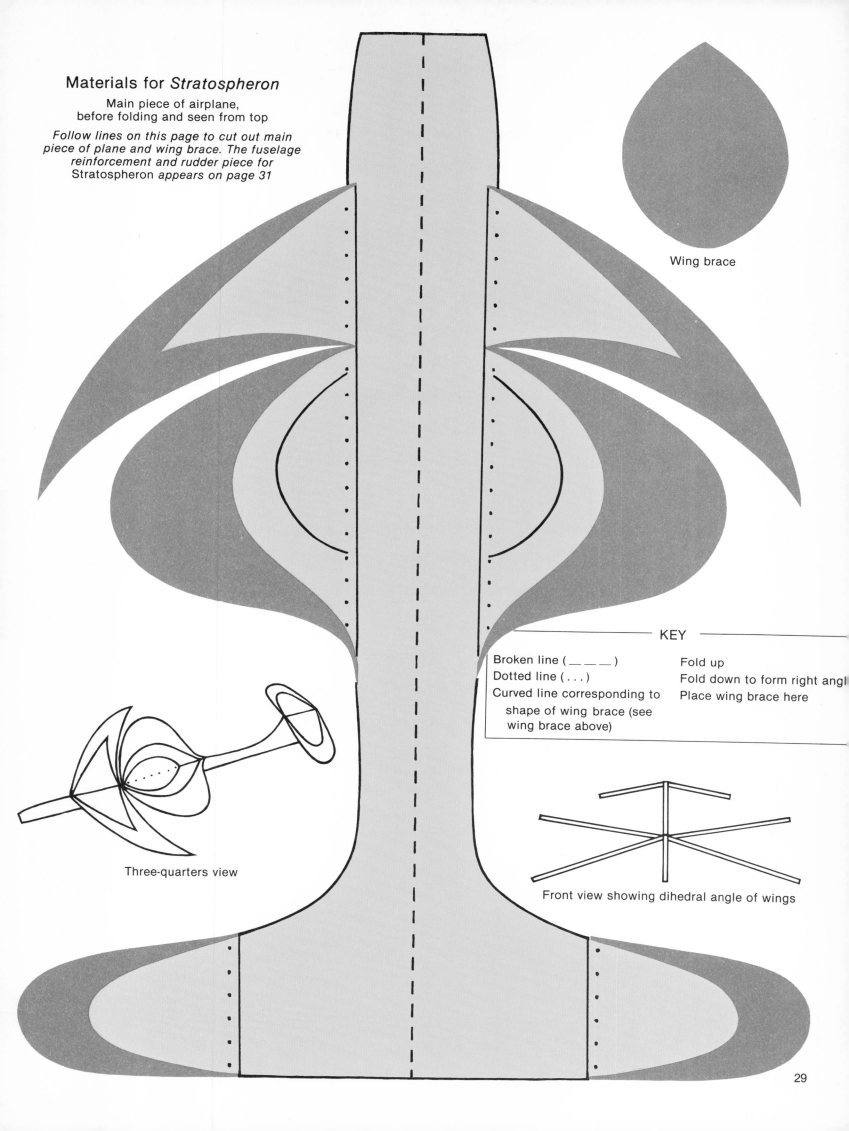

## Materials for *Stratospheron*

Main piece of airplane,
before folding and seen from top

*Follow lines on this page to cut out main
piece of plane and wing brace. The fuselage
reinforcement and rudder piece for
Stratospheron appears on page 31*

Wing brace

Three-quarters view

#### KEY

Broken line ( _ _ _ )  Fold up

Dotted line ( . . . )  Fold down to form right angl

Curved line corresponding to  Place wing brace here
  shape of wing brace (see
  wing brace above)

Front view showing dihedral angle of wings

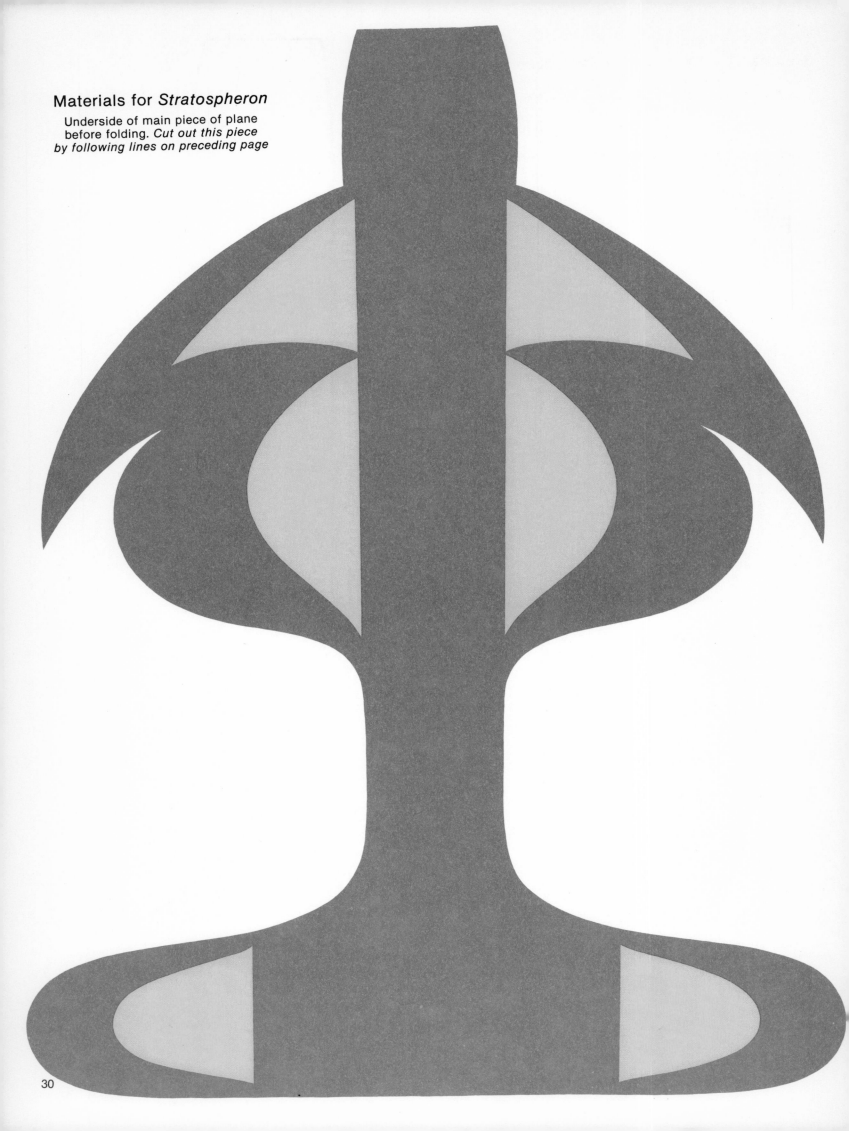

## Materials for *Stratospheron*

Underside of main piece of plane
before folding. *Cut out this piece
by following lines on preceding page*

## Materials for *Phantom* and *Stratospheron*

*Follow lines on this page to cut out
the fuselage reinforcement and rudder pieces
for* Phantom *and* Stratospheron

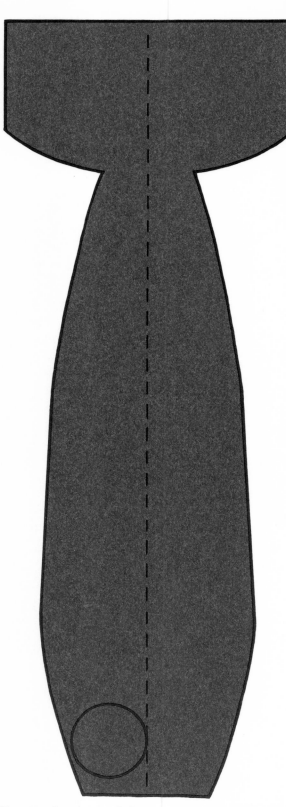

*Phantom* fuselage reinforcement and rudder piece

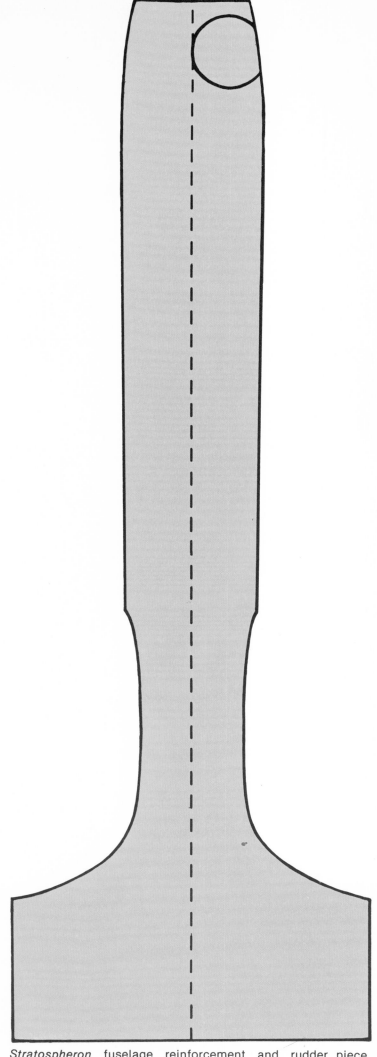

*Stratospheron* fuselage reinforcement and rudder piece.

---

**KEY**

Circle                     Place penny here
Broken line ( _ _ _ )      Fold up (and glue with penny inside)